To: Al Rice
My very best wishes
Melvin @ Noovaa
11/2/2002

They Never
CAME
BACK

HOW TO LOSE PATIENTS

Melvin A. Noonan, D.D.S., M.S.

TIMBRITOM PRESS
Birmingham, Michigan

Published by TIMBRITOM
P.O. Box 802
Birmingham, Michigan 48012-0802

Publisher's Cataloging-in-Publication Data
Noonan, Melvin, A.
    They never came back: how to lose patients / Melvin A. Noonan
    – Birmingham, Mich.: Timbritom, 1999.
        p.   ill.   cm.
    ISBN 0-9665934-0-5
    1. Noonan, Melvin, A. 2. Dentists—United States—Biography.
    3. Pedodontics. I. Title.

RK43 .N66 A3	1999	98-96363
617.6'0092	[B]—dc21	CIP

PROJECT COORDINATION BY JENKINS GROUP, INC.

03 02 01 00 ◆ 5 4 3 2 1

Printed in the United States of America

*This book is dedicated to my wife, Laurene, and
our three sons, Tim, Brian, and Tom,
who were always an inspiration, and who shared me
with dentistry, sometimes reluctantly.*

Contents

CONTENTS

SECTION TWO:
CHARACTERS I HAVE KNOWN

SECTION THREE:
OTHER STORIES FROM THE PRACTICE OF DENTISTRY

CONTENTS

Acknowledgments

*T*he author thanks the *Oakland County Dental Review*, where these stories first appeared, for permission to retell them here; and Elizabeth Jenkins, Barbara Daniel, and Dee Lyons for their constructive criticism and typing skills.

"We learn from our mistakes ... and most of us never lack for study tools."

— Author Unknown

Introduction

*T*he late Dr. Walter C. McBride, a pioneer in pediatric dentistry, was a mentor and very good friend of mine. He was the author of the first text book on pediatric dentistry and the first president of the American Society for Dentistry for Children.

One day, over lunch, he related to me his intention to write a book on interesting and entertaining events that happened during his years of practice. The title would be *Open Wider, Please.*

However, when he retired and time came to write, he said he could not recall enough episodes to create a book, although he knew there would have been plenty, if he had only recorded them when they happened.

Today, I find myself in almost the same situation. But I have been fortunate to have had the impetus of a periodic deadline provided by the publication of the *Oakland County Dental Review*, a publication of Michigan's Oakland County Dental Society. For more than ten years, I have been turning out brief monthly vignettes for this newsletter. These items have elicited many favorable comments from dentists and non-dentists alike, and many of my readers have urged me to seek broader publication because of what they perceive as timeless messages with a universal appeal.

I have written about the foibles and perils of dentistry: children's antics; patients who never came back; mentors; peers; character sketches; insights into dentists' marketing practices, or "what makes a good dentist"; and changes in my own viewpoints over the years.

Occasionally, I write about experiences unrelated to dentistry, with the mature perspective one has only after a work life of many years.

And so, I offer these "snapshots" of events; some of them can be digested almost at a glance . . . often with a chuckle . . . often with nostalgia.

What Is a Pedodontist?

*I*n 1949, I opened my office in a small house on Bates Street in Birmingham, Michigan, which the previous renter, a physician, had converted to professional space. It was a cute, red-brick cottage that was probably 100 years old at that time. To make it more attractive, I had it relandscaped. By doing so, the landlord generously extended my lease.

I had a sign especially made for me and mounted it on a lamppost. It was cut out of heavy-gauge metal and was a silhouette of a boy and a girl roller skating, and a dog running between them. The blacksmith had produced a real work of art.

Two plates hung from that portion by metal links. On the upper plate, I proudly displayed my name, M. A. Noonan, D.D.S. On the lower leaf was the word "PEDODONTIST." These plates could swing freely with the wind. It was truly a unique sign — the only one in the world like it. It was positioned near the sidewalk and close to the door to my private office.

It didn't take me long before I realized that not many natives of the town knew what a pedodontist was.

A few weeks after I placed the sign, an elderly woman entered and asked to see the doctor. You guessed it. She had problems with her feet. Now I could understand that. One could easily mistake PEDODONTIST for PODIATRIST . . . (leave the sign there; they will learn.)

By design, I was able to sit at my desk in the private office and, if the outer door was open, I could hear passersby talking.

On one occasion, two well-dressed women were walking by and stopped at the sign.

One said to the other, "What is a PED-O-DONTIST?"

The other replied, "I don't know, but it probably means something dirty."

That evening, the only leaf hanging was M.A. NOONAN, D.D.S.

Younger practitioners fought desperately to change the designation of the speciality to PEDIATRIC DENTISTRY, and succeeded. I personally felt that their reason was that they couldn't spell PEDODONTICS. But maybe they didn't want people to think they were doing something dirty.

Section One

How To Lose Patients

We Learn From Our Mistakes

*D*r. Jonah Salk once was told that he had made well over two hundred failures before he tasted success. He replied that he didn't recall any failures because he learned something from each try.

Today, many clinicians try to impress us with their successful cases when, in reality, they may have had very few. As an audience, we might be able to learn more if they presented their failures.

This applies to the management of a dental practice also. I feel certain that some of the so-called "authorities" on this subject are living off their honoraria and not from the income of a successful practice.

If my assumption is true — that we can learn from mistakes — I'm going to confess some of those that occurred during my thirty-eight years of pediatric dental practice. I learned from them, and they might help you.

Hopefully, you will enjoy these "confessions" and can relate to the situations presented and learn from them.

> "Failure is the opportunity to begin again
> more intelligently."
>
> — HENRY FORD

They Never Came Back

*M*any times during my years of dental practice, I wished I could speak several languages. Anyone practicing where I did has had patients who knew little English and some who knew none at all.

I recall once sitting on the floor of my operatory next to a Japanese mother going through a Japanese-English dictionary. It was time-consuming but fun. We were able to communicate enough so that I could treat the child to the satisfaction of both patient and parent. A smile can send a big message.

In another case, I was not successful in getting my message across . . .

A foreign woman came to the office with her child and she had a very severe case of body odor. She had on a black dress which she must have worn for months. Her English vocabulary was practically nil.

Knowing we all have off-days, I tried desperately to ignore the fumes and act professionally.

On her second trip to the office, another parent of a patient refused to remain in the reception room with her. She asked if I would allow her to wait in my private office. She could not tolerate the odor of the woman in the black dress.

Knowing that traditions, customs, and environment are different in different countries, I decided to try to help this woman fit into our society.

I tried desperately to tell her she had an offensive problem. She didn't understand. She did not know words such as "body odor," "deodorant," "perfume," or "soap." I tried everything short of holding my nose and pointing to her axilla.

In desperation, I held up the prescription pad. I was in luck. She knew what that was! So I wrote a prescription. We smiled and she left with it held tightly in her hand.

I have often wondered what the pharmacist thought when she presented a prescription: RX "Right Guard!"

I never found out, because . . . they never came back.

How To Lose Patients

*O*n one carefree day, an elderly looking woman brought a very cute four-year-old girl into my office. The rapport between the child and me was excellent. It was love at first sight. All was going well until I smilingly said, "You had grandmother bring you for moral support."

With that remark, the woman fired a curt reply, "I am her mother!"

The lesson I learned is that no matter how old the lady was, I should have referred to her as "mother" as in this case she was; then no offense.

On the other hand, if she was the grandmother and I had referred to her as "mother," she would have been so flattered she would have dragged all of her grandchildren into my practice.

Instead . . . *they never came back!*

You will always fare better in life if you underestimate the age of a woman.

We Don't Deliver Babies

I possess a genuine phobia for any part of obstetrics. I admire men who can remain in the delivery room and witness the wonders of nature. Not me. My wife was on her own for each of our three sons.

Whenever a pregnant woman was in my office, I had the fear that she would decide to have her unborn delivered there. I can assure you that one cry of pain from her would have had me out the back door before the receptionist could dial 911.

I recall vividly one incident which gave me much embarrassment.

A young mother was escorted into the operatory where I was

examining her daughter. The child needed another appointment for a couple of simple restorations.

When I turned to face the mother, I noticed her abdomen extended well beyond the point where the buttons on her coat would have contacted the intended button holes.

I said, "Mary has a few more problems and will need another appointment. I suggest we do it as soon as possible, but please tell me — when are you scheduled for delivery?"

Her reply: "I had the baby two weeks ago."

It was then I learned a diagnosis should not be made without good case history.

THEY NEVER CAME BACK!

They Never Came Back...
It's Contagious

I have often requested other dentists to share experiences in their practices which resulted in the loss of the patient.

Dr. Bruce Turpin related this story about his dad, Dr. Robert Turpin, who is now retired. The incident occurred during the age of the belt-driven handpiece. A very dignified patient was seated in his dental chair and, during the operative procedures, the belt caught the patient's hair! Lo and behold! It was not natural hair! The patient's toupee began making the trip around the course of the belt.

How frightened Robert must have been — thinking he would be charged with scalping his own patient. And the patient? You can well-imagine his embarrassment and understand the beating his ego had suffered. It is reported that after freeing his "rug," he left and never returned.

The moral of the story — do not UNCOVER family secrets.

The Broken Appointment

One of the most irritating situations in the practice of dentistry is the broken appointment.

Most patients do respect our time, but there are some who couldn't care less.

I tried desperately to prevent that from happening in my practice. I informed new patients of my policy to charge for broken appointments unless they gave a 24-hour notice. My appointment slips, which were in duplicate, carried the same message. The duplicates were filed in the patient's chart for later verification if that became necessary.

Common sense (which is not so common) will tell you that there are times beyond the control of a patient when it is impossible to keep the allotted time. This is understandable, and good judgment tells one to overlook these situations.

But there are others who keep appointments only if they cannot find anything else to do.

I never made a charge for the first missed trip, but reminded the parent of the policy. After that, the charge was posted. Good patients understood and paid. Yes, there really are people like that, but not enough, it seems.

On one occasion, after three broken appointments, the father refused to pay. Normally, you would forget it if he promised to go elsewhere. You lose money by keeping this type of person. But this man became abusive over the policy, so I felt it was time to fight for a principle. I took him to court.

The judge ruled in my favor. He mentioned the fact that he had been charged and paid for a broken appointment.

The defendant had to pay the broken appointment charge and court costs. You KNOW he never came back.

The moral of the story is to pick a friendly judge if you want to try this. In this case, his honor's children were patients of mine and HE had paid me for a broken appointment.

Don't Mix Friends
With Patients

I was never certain if it was a good policy to make patients out of friends or friends out of patients. If things didn't work well, you could be a double loser. One such example comes to mind.

George was a high school classmate of mine and a real nice guy. I looked up to him. He was very athletic and involved in varsity sports. I, on the other hand, looked like the perfect example of malnutrition and my only chance for a school letter was in cheerleading. Even that I didn't do well, due to a lack of coordination plus the frail frame.

When I opened my practice in Birmingham, Michigan, George was one of the first people to call for an appointment for his child. Here was my chance to have him look up to me. He couldn't do dentistry, but I could.

On each appointment, we enjoyed reminiscing over our high school days, which was great. But after each trip, it took three statements to have him send his check. The first was the regular one, the second had "second notice" typed on it, and the third was stamped in red ink, "final notice."

After this pattern of payment continued over a couple of years, I decided to change it. After the child's next recall, the first statement had "final notice" across the face. The next day the phone rang and it was George. He related that he had received the statement and thought there was an error. "It was marked 'final notice' and this is the first one I have received," he said.

I replied, "That is correct, George. You have always waited to receive the final notice before paying, so I thought I could save two mailings by placing 'final notice' on the first one."

I have never seen George since. To this day, I might be enjoying his company had he not decided to be a patient of mine.

False Identity

One of many mistakes I made during my years of practice is rather embarrassing to admit. Although I am reluctant to confess it, it was a learning experience for me, so I'll pass it on.

During a hectic day at the office, I entered the operatory. The assistant had placed the three-year-old child in the chair, bib in place, tray set, and all ready for me to go.

After greeting the youngster, I checked the film and chart. There was my assignment — an incipient carious lesion on the proximal surface of S___. I administered the anesthetic and proceeded to make idle talk with the patient while waiting for the results of the injection.

When the lip became numb, it was time to start.

As any dentist well knows, one can do an ideal preparation on a tooth with very little decay. I did just that. It was as close to perfect as I could make it. I was just reaching for the matrix when my hygienist came sliding into the room and said, "You have the wrong patient. She was only here for a recall and scheduled for me. I have your patient."

Now I ask you, "Have you ever had instant diarrhea?" That is the exact feeling I had when I realized the mistake. I had prepared a perfectly normal tooth in a caries-free mouth.

The only honorable thing to do was to tell the child's father. He seemed to be a good sport and accepted my explanation of the mix-up. There was nothing else to do but continue and restore the tooth. After that, the hygienist did the prophylaxis for which the child had been scheduled.

When I dismissed the patient, I told the father in a facetious tone, "There is no charge for the restoration your child didn't need, and all the other services rendered are 'on the house.' "

We both laughed, but he was not the one sweating. He seemed very understanding and accepted my mistake and apology gracefully. But they NEVER CAME BACK.

When I questioned my assistant about how she could place the wrong child in my dental chair, she explained that the child had responded to the wrong name and the father watched her walk in.

I assure you it never happened again. At that point, I seriously considered instituting a positive identifying system using fingerprints.

The Acid Attack

A colleague who allowed me to use his name related an incident that happened to him during the treatment of a dapper gentleman. Tom Vestevich, upon his discharge from the military service, did general practice before he became an orthodontist.

The patient was in the chair and Tom was proceeding to do endodontics on a lower anterior. The procedure was going along smoothly, but Tom had committed a cardinal sin. He had placed an open bottle of phenol on the tray . . . you can guess the results.

The patient's knee struck the tray and the bottle tipped. A goodly amount of the acid poured on the patient's leg.

All procedures were put on hold and the patient was sent into the private office where he removed his pants. The acid had gone through the trousers and contacted the skin. The leg was washed and the acid neutralized, but the pant leg was destroyed. Now what to do?

It was a unanimous decision that the damaged pant leg had to be cut off. You can well imagine how the poor patient looked with one short and one long pant leg.

The appearance did not meet with anyone's approval. So a second decision was made to cut off the other leg. (I should mention that the pants, which now were shorts, were part of a three-piece suit.)

Tom completed the dental treatment and, being a generous man, wrote a check that would more than cover the cost of the suit. The man accepted the check but stalled long enough to gain courage before he left the office in his newly created outfit.

Tom and his staff expressed sadness and sympathy until the patient was out of ear contact. Then — and only then — stimulated by the sight of the poor guy's appearance as he left the office, a shock wave of uncontrollable laughter overcame them.

Whenever anyone asks Tom about the incident, he still breaks up.

Incidentally . . . the patient NEVER CAME BACK.

The "Fee" Thing

*H*ave you ever lost a patient due to your fees? Say "no" to that, and I will call you a prevaricator of the highest degree. I am a firm believer that there are some people out there who would complain if you did the work free.

I had not been in practice very long before I experienced an irate mother of one of my patients. She insisted on giving me some motherly advice.

"Young man, you are not going to last long in this town because you charge too much. You think because the citizens of Birmingham have a reputation of having above-the-average income, you can overcharge." (At that time, a class II amalgam went for $4.00.)

I thought to myself, "Okay, lady, you said it; but I'll convince you my fees are very fair. And when I'm through, you will still be a patient of mine."

I stated in a calm and pleasant voice, "I think you are being unfair. Do you have any idea what expense I went through to establish this office? Do you have any idea what my rent is? Do you have any idea what the supplies cost? Do you have any idea what my payroll is? Do you have any idea what my utilities cost? Now be truthful with me. How can you say my fees are too high without considering these facts? Let me put it another way: What basis would you use to establish a fee if you were me?"

Instead of a calming effect, she became more emotional and said, "You sound like Detroit Edison."

My reply: "Thank you for the compliment. I consider Edison an efficient, successful operation."

She turned without a word, left and NEVER CAME BACK.

I look back with much trepidation, thinking of what would happen if you reduced your fees every time someone complained.

The Envelope Caper

All of us are dependent on others to some degree. But there is a great mass of people who feel that the world owes them a living and that they must be catered to.

I have always felt that when I treated a patient, I was obligated to do the best dentistry that my ability allowed. When I extended credit, they should be obligated to me. After all, I was not a financial institution. I didn't charge interest; they should consider that fact a favor and appreciate it. Most did. I cared for them; they cared for me.

Occasionally, there was that "you must do everything for me" type. Hiam Ginott, in his book, *Between Parent and Child*, states, "Where there is dependence, there is hostility." In one such case, I can prove his point.

A new patient came to my office, and I completed all the necessary treatments. The child was placed on my recall list and a statement sent at the end of the month.

Payment was made promptly, but accompanying the check was a curt note stating, "Send return envelopes with your statements."

I felt that the return envelope was his obligation (after all, I had extended him enough courtesy), so I ignored the note.

After the six-month recall visit, another statement was sent, and again without a return envelope. Once again, a note came with the check, stating, "Evidently you wish to ignore my request for return envelopes."

I felt compelled to answer that one. So, with pen in hand, I responded:

> Dear Sir:
>
> You and I have something in common. We hate to supply envelopes for each other. So, I have a plan whereby you need not use an envelope of yours nor do I have to supply one of mine. It is a very simple plan: Pay before you leave the office. Not only will each of us save an envelope, but also postage.
>
> Hopefully, you will agree to this.
>
> Sincerely, . . .

In this case, Ginott was correct. His dependence on me created hostility. THEY NEVER CAME BACK.

From THOSE Who "KNOW"

Preventive dentistry is or should be a concern for all of us. We preach it daily. The regular patients in one's practice understand and appreciate the interest we demonstrate in keeping their oral health at peak level.

Every patient in my practice was taught to properly care for their teeth. My "sermon" to all new patients included proper brushing, flossing, and diets. I carefully explained the reasons for, and value of, radiographs and other necessary treatments, and included the importance of regular check-ups.

Those of normal intelligence understood and followed my instructions; but on occasion, there was the intelligent patient with a warped sense of values.

A patient of record and her mother had visited my office on a regular basis for approximately two years. Both were friendly and easy to deal with.

On the child's fourth recall appointment, the father joined them. He was a rather aggressive man, and questioned the benefit of my seeing his daughter every six months.

Here was my chance to educate this man (who, by the way, was an attorney) to the benefits of prevention. I took the time to explain that the program available to his daughter at my office was a great benefit and a good investment in her health. All during this discussion, I tried to project a warm and friendly attitude.

Did I sell it? Did he buy it? The answer to both is "No." To the embarrassment of his wife, he stated that the prevention package was none other than a money-making scheme. He told me that he only visited his dentist every two years to have his teeth cleaned.

One glance at his teeth would even impress a lay person that he was long overdue for a thorough prophylaxis. His arrogance made it a challenging situation;

So I replied, "Sir, to be perfectly honest with you, your teeth appear as though you have not seen a dentist within five years."

At that point, I was certain that I had seen the last of his child. And so it was — they never came back.

A few weeks after that appointment, he sent a check for half of the fee; and written on the face was, "Paid in full."

It was not worth the effort to seek the full amount so I closed the file on that case. But I felt compelled to strike back, so I purchased what I felt was an appropriate card. Its message read, "Sorry to hear you are sick — hope you recover soon."

Believe me, I took great pleasure in signing my name to that one.

The Voice of Control

After 38 years of specialization in pediatric dentistry, I assure you that the behavior patterns of children in a dental situation showed great improvement between the time I started and when I hung up the handpiece for good.

Most of the credit can be given to "prevention." The results of therapeutic fluorides and the attention given to patient education have improved the oral health of children. The child patient has less to fear when visiting a dentist.

In earlier years, a great percentage of patients were referred to the specialists because they were behavior-management problems.

I recall a boy of five years who was referred to me as a problem child. He had been able to fight his way out of four different dental offices.

On the initial appointment, he presented no problems. I was able to examine him, take radiographs, and present the treatment plan to the mother without one issue. I was amazed.

The second appointment was quite different. The receptionist brought him from the reception room without any objection from him. He stopped at the side of the chair and told me he was not getting in. With that stated, he started to scream and run for the exit.

I caught him, placed him into the chair firmly, raised my voice over his screams and said, "You are not going to act like that in my office."

He was startled. He stopped the noise and stared at me with wide-open eyes.

Then in a calm voice, I explained that I needed his cooperation for the tasks at hand. I wanted to be his friend and hoped he would be mine. I extended my hand in a friendly gesture and we shook hands.

Then with friendly chatter, I proceeded with the local anaesthetic and completed the necessary operative procedures. I complimented the young man and all was well between us. I was proud.

I invited the mother in to view the restorations and be informed as to how well her son had done. She didn't come to the chair. Instead, she stopped at the door and with fire in her eyes, she said, "You raised your voice to my child!"

I stated, "That is correct. I raise my voice to my own children when it is necessary."

Her reply: "He was never afraid of a dentist before."

I remarked facetiously, "He is now!"

She didn't accept it as humor!

You could have guessed — THEY NEVER CAME BACK!

I have often wondered if the dentist who saw him after that ever threatened with, "If you don't behave, I'll send you back to Noonan."

The Third-Party Triangle

*W*hen prepaid dental insurance took roots in the dental profession, I decided to change my practice to a pay-as-you-go basis. Patients would have to pay after each treatment; no more statements.

I agreed to complete the insurance forms and send them to the insurance company. The carrier would reimburse the patient. Not being a financial institution, I felt this to be fair. The patient would have some financial obligation.

After all — the employer paid the premium, the patient received the benefit, and the insurance company made the profit. Where did that leave me? . . . on the pay-as-you-go basis; and I liked it. Sorry to say, not all of my patients agreed.

One such parent was an executive employed by General Motors. He came to my office with a copy of a letter that I had sent to all of my patients explaining my new policy.

He stated that I didn't understand how the third-party payment plan worked. He continued to tell me that when the insurance form for the patient was completed and submitted to the insurance company, they would send me a check, and then I should bill him for the balance. He wanted no financial responsibility other than the small balance.

I restated my position, telling him it was just a question of whose money we were going to use. After all, I had expenses which had to be paid before the insurance check arrived. He told me that General Motors said it should be done his way.

I replied, "Sir, if I wanted G.M. to tell me how to run my practice, I would be employed by them. Thankfully, I am not." At that point, it was obvious his children would be on the list of former patients who NEVER CAME BACK!

I am certain that my work load was somewhat reduced by this plan. But happily, most of my patients willingly accepted the plan and cooperated.

Faulty Reception

After retiring from private practice, I was hired as the Executive Director of the Oakland County Dental Society; and in this position, I was called upon to listen to complaints from irate patients of some of our members. I can honestly say that 90 percent of these problems stem from a lack of communication, a misunderstanding or even misinterpretation of a word.

There is a small portion of the population to whom, when you say, "Good morning," they wonder what you meant by that.

Clear communications are especially important when you are treating the child patient. Terminology must be selected carefully. I never used words like "shot" or "needle." I replaced them in my vocabulary with "injection" and "syringe" — words which the patients found much less frightening.

I always felt that it was imperative to explain all of the procedures to a young patient before attempting any treatment. I showed them how I used the mirror to see their teeth. I demonstrated the explorer on my fingernail and then on theirs. I explained the handpiece by telling them it sounded like a jet airplane. I would let them hold it over the cuspidor and engage the switch.

This system of "inform before you perform" worked very well on most patients . . . but not all. One of the new patients did not respond to our six-month recall notice. The family also ignored the second reminder. The receptionist followed up with a telephone call and was greeted with, "I wouldn't take my child back to that man. He frightened the hell out of him. He threatened to stick a jet airplane in his mouth."

There are times you cannot win for losing, and this was one where THEY NEVER CAME BACK. What you imply is not always what they infer.

The Dealer's Hand … uh … Family

*I*n the practice of dentistry, you will gain patients who are in business and want to sell their products to you. "I do business with you; you do business with me." I see nothing wrong with that unless you have two patients in the same business. The problem: Which one do I deal with?

Several children in my practice had parents who were automobile dealers. When I reached that point in life where the family needed a second car, I considered several economy ones.

My final choice was a German-made Volkswagen "Beetle." I loved it. It served me well and I enjoyed driving it.

On one occasion, I was seen driving it by another parent in my practice who was a Ford dealer. He remarked, "I didn't know you were a German dentist."

"No," I replied, "I'm not a German dentist, but I would rather buy a product from Germany than to have my tax dollars go to foreign aid."

Your assumption is correct. I never saw him in my office again.

What did this experience teach me? I learned that if you have to choose between patients when you are doing business, always pick the one with the largest family. In this case, the Ford dealer only had one child; the Volkswagen dealer had six.

Don't Judge a Book By Its Cover

*I*t has been said that you cannot tell a man by the clothes he wears. I have experienced many occasions in life to prove that to be true. One of those experiences happened in my practice. There was a classy-appearing couple who brought their two youngsters to me for several years. The son was handsome and the daughter was a future candidate for Miss America.

After each appointment, the mother would open her purse and retrieve the amount of cash necessary to pay the charge. The peculiar thing about this was that the bills in her purse were not arranged in any order, but looked like they had been placed in there as if one would take a handful of lettuce and just stuff it in.

Although a receipt was made for each cash transaction, the mother would take it and immediately deposit it in the nearest waste basket.

I never had any inkling of what business they were in and I didn't care. They were excellent patients.

After one of their recall appointments, the mother stated that she was unable to pay at that time because their bar had been burned completely. With their track record, I didn't hesitate to tell her she could pay when they got squared away and I wouldn't bother them.

They returned on the next recall and the mother cleared their account in the same fashion — unfolding bills that had been jammed into the purse.

Shortly after that appointment, I read in the newspaper that the father became an auto-parts distributor by just turning on the ignition key. Parts of his car were distributed all over his neighborhood . . . along with parts of his body.

The article further stated that he was involved in a "chop shop" deal which I understand is not legal. For those of you who do not know what a "chop shop" is, let me explain. It is a branch of organized crime which steals cars and trucks, dismantles them and sells the parts for more than the vehicle is worth whole. Their specialty was to dismantle big truck tractors. Their only mistake was to dissect one that belonged to someone else in the same type of illegal operation.

My office sent the recall card for the children's appointments on the proper date, but it was returned, stamped by the post office: "Unable to deliver — no forwarding address."

THEY NEVER CAME BACK.

A Religious Issue

*H*earing that I had reached my limit on recalling "they never came back" incidents, one of our orthodontists volunteered one of his. He offered to tell me, however, only if I promised not to divulge his name. So, being a man of my word, I'll just refer to him as Dr. John Doe.

A parent had brought a new patient to Dr. Doe's office for consultation. The family impressed him as very refined people. He examined the child and found the case one that would be relatively easy to treat; the kind that makes an orthodontist look like a genius without much effort on his part. The mother accepted the treatment plan very readily and was even agreeable to the fee quoted.

Then Dr. Doe, with chart in hand, started to guide the parent to the front desk where the necessary appointments could be scheduled. On the way, the mother said, "By the way, are you any relation to Henry Doe?"

His reply, "I know Henry, but we are not related; as a matter of fact, we don't even go to church on the same day." He thought this remark humorous.

The mother stopped, looked him in the eye, and said, "Henry Doe is our next-door neighbor and a very close friend. Our family thinks very highly of him."

With that stated, she continued to walk past the front desk and through the front door with her child tagging along. They never returned.

Now I ask you, "Is that a learning experience?" It should be. NEVER JOKE ABOUT DIFFERENCES IN RELIGION!

What Goes Around, Comes Around

I wrote earlier about the decision I made when buying a second car. There was a Ford dealer and a Volkswagen dealer in my practice. From whom should I purchase a car? I concluded that the second auto would only be transportation to and from the office and other local spots.

The Volkswagen would serve that purpose very well and leave a lot more room in my garage. So, that was my choice.

The Ford dealer saw me driving the VW in town and discontinued bringing his only child to my office. That was a loss, but it would have been a greater loss had the VW dealer left. He had five children in my practice.

Recently, in a physician's reception room, a very neat young gentleman asked if I was Dr. Noonan. I answered in the affirmative. When he told me his name, I recalled he was the son of the Ford dealer.

In the course of our friendly conversation, I asked what he was doing for a living. He told me he was working for Volkswagen. I chuckled and told him why his dad had discontinued bringing him to my office.

Then I inquired about his parents. He stated that his dad had retired and was living in Traverse City, Michigan. "And by the way," he said, "Dad now drives a Volkswagen."

We have all heard the statement, "What goes around, comes around." Now I have reason to believe it.

Loss of (Referral) Status

*J*ust when you think you have heard it all, along comes another true story that is really different and difficult to believe. Another of our prominent orthodontists sent it to me (seems like they have all the fun). Word for word, I relate the story.

"A general dentist in my area with a large, active practice, including associate dentists, inexplicably stopped referring patients to my orthodontic office for either consultation and/or treatment. This dentist, whom I had known for over a decade, both professionally and socially, actually referred to me as his *best* friend.

"One noon, when this professional colleague and 'friend,' who routinely joined me for lunch, stopped at my office, I summoned enough nerve and courage to pointedly ask him why he and his office had stopped referring any patients to my office. Without hesitation, this dentist replied, 'Because you're not divorced!'

"In amazement, I asked what he meant by that remark.

"This dentist explained that since he went through his own divorce, he had to feel sorry for the other three orthodontists in this area, all of whom were divorced! I really shouldn't feel too bad, he explained, because he selected other dental specialists on the same basis of whether they were divorced or not.

"When I told him that this was truly unfair and unprofessional, he stated, '. . . not being divorced, you really don't need the money; and if you ever do get divorced, I'll start referring patients to you again.'

"I asked — then insisted — that this man leave my office. Bewildered at my insistence, he finally left and never returned."

My advice is to evaluate this case very carefully before you consider changing your marital status. It may be more profitable to lose the referrals.

Twenty percent of men kiss their wife goodbye when they leave their house. Eighty percent kiss their house goodbye when they leave their wife.

— Author Unknown

Never Err . . . At a Low Level

As I confessed before, I made many errors in my years of practice, and all honest practitioners (and often the general public) can relate to some of those or other incidents that may have embarrassed them. One occurred to a friend of mine. It was awkward, but humorous.

My friend had a patient in his practice who would not sit in the dental chair unless he was served a good shot of bourbon. This was routine ritual for the man. He allowed enough time before his appointment to swallow his liquid courage and to relax.

On one appointment, after his stress level was reduced, the receptionist called him. He walked to the operatory where he was greeted by Dr. Doe. They shook hands, he glanced around, but did not sit in the chair. Instead, he turned and walked back to the reception desk and asked for another appointment.

The doctor followed and asked why he wanted another appointment.

The patient stated, "You are not working on me today. You are drunker than I am. Look at your feet!"

Lo and behold! When the doctor checked his feet, he had on one brown shoe and one black shoe.

The patient did leave after selecting another date, and the doctor took much more care in dressing himself thereafter.

Don't Open The "Cover"

A very good friend and a classmate of mine practiced pedodontics in Detroit for quite a few years before he accepted a position on the dental faculty of Southern California University. He has a great sense of humor and sees the funny side of every situation. We had many chuckles discussing situations we had experienced in our own offices.

We also shared the same philosophy. Rarely would we allow the parent in the operatory during dental procedures. We both felt that we were experts at handling children but very inept at handling parents.

A parent in the room was a distraction for the child. Their presence diluted our authority with the patient. When you gave a command, the child would turn to the parent for approval to follow or not follow the order.

On the other side of the coin, if the parent was a cute young mother, it was a definite distraction for the operator.

On one occasion, my friend was treating a young patient who was cooperating very well and all systems were "go." It was another of those perfect sessions where both patient and doctor were relaxed and contented.

When the procedures were completed, my friend went to the reception room door to invite the mother in to show and explain the treatment he had just completed. When he opened the door, the mother, who had held her head pressed against the door to listen, fell flat on her face at his feet.

He knew by the look in her eyes and the degree of embarrassment she displayed, that she would never return; and SO IT WAS.

At times, you just cannot win for losing . . . but this is one sure method to have the parent look up to you.

A Difference Of Opinion

I was taught early in my professional career that you never talked religion or politics to patients unless you were very certain that they shared your same philosophies. At one time in history, it was safe to talk about motherhood and apple pie. Everybody agreed. But today, even those topics are not safe ones.

There is disagreement over motherhood, and about the cholesterol in pie crust.

Recently, a member who wishes to remain anonymous, reported a story that proves the old philosophy stated above is still correct.

One of our members, who is well respected and has a fine reputation for the quality of dental care he provides, is also a very conservative person.

His hero is none other than Rush Limbaugh. He tries desperately not to miss a show of Limbaugh's. As a matter of fact, he keeps a radio in his laboratory and has the volume high enough so he can hear good ole' Rush while doing dentistry.

On a certain day, a very respectable-looking woman had been seated in the dental chair. But before he entered the operatory, he checked the volume on the radio. He didn't want to miss a word.

When he greeted his patient, she asked, "Do you listen to him?" referring to Rush.

Well, our friend, in his opinion, extolled the virtues of Limbaugh. He felt strongly that if people would listen, Rush could save America.

"Is that right?" replied the good patient. Saying no more, she unclipped the bib, picked up her purse, and was out the door.

Rush may be able to save or correct some things in America, but on the other side of the coin, he has the ability to send some patients flying from your practice.

Maybe the safest programs to be piped into your office are music stations. Even then, remember that you will never please them all.

The (Not So) Healing "Touch"

*I*t is difficult to realize that there are cases where abuse can be inflicted on children of a so-called civilized society. We must do our part to try to eliminate this malady from our culture.

However, with all the publicity this subject has gained, it makes one feel uncomfortable when expressing friendship in an innocent manner. A friendly pat on the head or back may be interpreted by a sick mind as child molesting. I can relate one such case that happened in my practice.

A female patient, age five, had been coming to my office for two years and we never had a problem. Then one day it happened. She was reluctant to have a small restoration placed, and her mother had to walk her into the operatory. She climbed into the chair unassisted, put her head down and started to cry.

I gently and lightly tapped her in the ribs with my index finger and said, "Now you are not going to act like that today, are you?"

The mother spoke up and said, "Do you always *fondle* children?"

I could not believe my ears. Was this a bad dream, or did I hear what I just thought I heard? I turned, looked at the mother, and realized she was not being facetious.

It was at this point that I lost my cool. I told the mother if she considered my action as fondling, she was really mentally sick and needed help. Her exit from the office was not fast enough to suit me, and I felt like a push would have been very appropriate.

I shudder even today to think what would have been the result had that woman tried to convince the police that I had molested her child.

It is indeed a strange world we live in when you become fearful of even smiling and saying "hello" to a youngster for fear it will be translated as a devious act. Be cautious when you hear that commercial, "Reach out and touch someone."

Just Do It My Way

On one occasion in my practice, a young mother brought in a patient of five years. The child was in need of several restorations and a space maintainer to replace a prematurely lost primary molar. During consultation, I explained the child's problems and the necessary procedures to correct the situation.

The parent agreed to what I proposed but stated that she wanted all gold restorations and a gold bridge instead of a spacer.

I told her that, although it was very impractical, I would be more than willing to do it her way, but it would be much more costly.

She replied, "Don't worry about costs. My ex-husband is responsible for the charges."

There was the clue. I learned early not to get involved in divorce cases. So I promptly contacted the child's father.

He seemed like a nice guy, and stated, "Go ahead and do it her way, but you will not get paid. She is trying to break me. She wants my blood. I'll pay for amalgams and the spacer, but nothing more."

Before the patient's next appointment, I contacted the mother and related the father's position. She became very irate when I stated that she would be responsible for the fees if she insisted on having gold. She canceled all appointments and I never saw her again.

I have often wondered if she was able to convince some other dentist to agree to her treatment plan. If she did, that dentist invested in a gold mine and lost it all.

The moral of the story: If you are told that someone else is responsible for the bill, check it out! You will save yourself a lot of grief.

～

The Unkindest Cut

A guaranteed method for reducing any professional's practice load is to embarrass the patients. One can do this easily to adults as well as children, but especially to children. They comprehend more than we give them credit for. On this subject, one case comes to mind.

An orthodontist friend of mine was sending his young daughter to a general practitioner whom he respected and who practiced in his building.

The child was a very shy and sensitive young girl with one notable flaw — poor dental hygiene. On her last trip to that dentist's office, the doctor was upset at the lack of care the patient had demonstrated after all of his previous lectures on oral hygiene. He felt that all of his efforts so far had failed, so he proceeded to shame her.

He brought in another young patient and her parent from the reception room and showed them the neglected mouth of the orthodontist's daughter.

He stated, "Would you believe that this girl's father is a dentist? I don't think she owns a toothbrush!"

How cruel! How cruel!

After that, I'm sure the girl paid more attention to oral hygiene, but it would have taken more than a Ferguson tractor to return her to that office. Not only did that doctor lose that family as patients, but he also destroyed any friendly ties he had with the orthodontist.

Even though it is frustrating to see the lack of care in a patient's oral cavity after all of your lectures and demonstrations, please be kind. Remember — you get more flies with honey!

Guilt By Association

As I have confessed, I lost patients from my practice for a variety of reasons. Many of these I can look back on with a chuckle. Nevertheless, they were learning experiences; and one should avoid making the same mistake twice.

But when you lose patients because you are a victim of circumstance, it is frustrating.

I had three very fine youngsters in my practice who would be a real asset to any dental office. The parents were well pleased with the service rendered and always paid promptly without question.

The parents were patients of another DDS who practiced in the same building. The mother's four upper anteriors were non-carious but unsightly. She was sold on the idea that porcelain jackets would improve her smile, and she selected that route to better esthetics. This was a wise choice, had she been in the hands of a competent operator.

When the jackets were inserted, the woman had pain but was told her discomfort would be only temporary. Instead, it continued to increase.

She sought other opinions and discovered that each of the teeth had become devital due to excessive removal of tooth structure. Each preparation was a near exposure, and pulpal therapy was necessary. The fee for this service only added insult to injury.

A short time after the treatments were completed, I met the woman in town and she related her story. Then she said, "I know it isn't fair to you. You had nothing to do with my problem, but I am not going to bring my children back to you. I don't even want to get near that building, and I surely don't know what I might do if I ran into him in the hall."

And so it was: I was a victim of circumstances. THEY NEVER CAME BACK.

It seemed to me that I had lost enough patients on my own; I really didn't need his help.

SECTION TWO

CHARACTERS I HAVE KNOWN

The Mechanical Wonder

A classmate of mine at the University of Detroit School of Dentistry and University of Michigan graduate school is a very good friend and interesting person. He was a salesperson's delight. He was enthusiastic about every new dental gadget on the market and first in the area to purchase it even though he would have it up for sale a month later.

Not only dental equipment, but automobiles. He was the first in our circle of friends to have a four-wheel-drive Jeep. This was back in 1948. It was the type used by the U.S. Army.

He took great pleasure in demonstrating how it would ride over curbs and could be parked in areas inaccessible to the average car. At times, he used it as a bulldozer to make room between two parked cars so he could fit it into the space.

He had more energy than any man I have ever known. He was a paratrooper during World War II, received his private pilot's license after the war and enjoyed an occasional ride on his motorcycle. But the one item that created the most laughter was his Izetta.

The Izetta was sold for a short time in this country around 1952. That being the case, most of you readers will not remember it. It was a small, weird-looking car. The oddest feature was that you entered the car from the front end. That is correct. The windshield and instrument panel were part of the door — the only door.

My friend learned very quickly that the front entrance was a handicap when parallel parking. On one occasion, after having lunch and going to the car, he could not get in because the car ahead had been parked too closely to allow him to enter his own. He had to go into several businesses along that strip until he found the owner of the car blocking his entry.

Another disadvantage was that the vehicle seemed to attract traffic police. They seemed to pick on him when he drove that car. When he finally reached the point where his driver's license was in jeopardy, he had to go to court. Pleading his own case, he told his story to the judge.

"When I drive my father's Buick, the police never bother me. But as soon as I drive off in the Izetta, flashing lights pull up behind me and I'm issued a traffic citation."

His Honor listened intently and then said, "That being the case, why don't you sell the silly damned thing?"

No Ducks

A character I know is a member of our dental society. He is an enthusiastic hunter. It is a very safe bet that you will never find him in his office during duck or deer season. In fairness to him, I shall not use his name. Besides being fair, I don't want to endanger my life. He is an excellent shot.

On one duck hunting venture a few years ago, he and his hunting partner, Ron, sat in the duck blind all day without having a bird come close enough to put a bead on it. They had not experienced a shutout very often in their many years of hunting together.

When they finally gave up, they decided to fire the shells in their shotguns instead of unloading. So they decided a plan for competition.

Our member stated that he would throw his hat and his partner could have one shot at it. Then in return, he would have one shot at his buddy's hat.

Agreed and ready to go, my colleague sailed his hat like a frisbee but just an inch above the ground. His partner pulled the trigger, a shot was heard and dirt flew up two inches behind the sailing hat. He had missed.

Now Ron was to throw his hat. He thought sailing it in the same fashion made it a difficult target, so he did likewise. Throwing it as hard as possible and as close to the ground as he could, he waited for the shot. But our member didn't shoot until it landed. He walked over to the hat and, at point-blank range, blew the hat to pieces. Nice trick!

Ron learned his lesson. When dealing with his hunting partner, you better get all the ground rules in writing.

(P.S. — they are still friends.)

A Gem In The ... Rubbish!

*T*he late George Marin was a great delight to know. It is truly unfortunate that my readers undoubtedly never knew him. He saw the humorous side of every situation and could embellish it every time he retold a story.

He always walked the three short blocks from his residence to his office. On a certain trash-collection day while on his way to work, he noticed a putter protruding from a trash can. Even though at first glance he felt it might help his golf score, it was beneath his dignity to have anyone see him picking through the rubbish.

He hastened his footsteps to his office, raced up the stairs, threw open the door and went directly to the telephone.

He called his wife, Marian, and ordered that she awaken their son, John, and have him dash to the trash can in front of the brown house and retrieve that putter before the trash man carried it off.

John's assignment was completed in short order even though his eyes were only half open.

George told that story with great delight and claimed that the resurrected putter did lower his score.

If he gets a copy of this article up in Heaven, he'll chuckle again.

Dangerous Misadventures

*K*en, a fraternity brother of mine during my days in under-graduate studies, certainly could be classified as a character. He has a fun-loving personality with a mind that is constantly concocting some humorous plot.

Years ago at a formal fraternity ball, he insisted — and pro-ceeded to demonstrate — how one could remove the tablecloth from a table fully set without disturbing the setting. One quick jerk of the cloth and his mission would be accomplished.

With confidence, he grabbed the cloth and gave the magic pull. Every item on the table crashed to the floor. He shook his head and said, "I don't know why it didn't work this time," and then left.

Those of us at the table had a good laugh on Ken but were left to clean up the mess.

In recent correspondence, he wrote the following: "I recent-ly had a close brush with death. A friend of mine coaxed me into going horseback riding. It has been more than thirty years since I have been on a horse. At first, things were going smoothly, but in a very short time I was thrown from the beast. The horse's steel-clad hooves were coming down within inches of my head. I was sure I would be killed and I would have been if the manager from Walmart had not rushed to my rescue and pulled the plug."

You have to love a character like that.

SECTION THREE

OTHER STORIES FROM THE PRACTICE OF DENTISTRY

The Phony Is Exposed

*I*n my introduction, I mentioned the name of one of my mentors, Dr. Walter C. McBride. He was the epitome of professionalism and a renowned national figure in the field of pediatric dentistry. He was a devoted crusader for improving the dental health of children. I felt very fortunate to have him as a role model.

McBride was one of the first tenants in the Fisher Building in Detroit when it opened its doors in 1928. Believe me — that was the top of the line; the cream of the profession practiced in that building.

I felt like my guardian angel was doing overtime in P.R. on my behalf when Walter called to see if I would take over his practice for three months in 1948 while he and his wife, Hilda, toured Europe.

I would have to interrupt my graduate training, but that wasn't all that bad. I needed the money. The state Board granted me a temporary specialty license and we made the deal.

McBride invited me to visit his office and observe his routine before he left on his tour. I will never forget the surprise I had while searching for suite 660. There was my name in gold leaf on the door — my childhood dream come true.

When he returned from his wandering in the Old World, McBride was impressed that I had more than filled my quota during his absence. He wanted me to join him in practice and was willing to let me write the ticket for our partnership. But, due to one experience I had in his office, I declined.

Upon his return and his first visit back to the office, McBride entered through the back door. He did this to avoid parents and patients waiting in the reception room, as he was not yet ready to inform them that he was available.

The young patient on whom I was operating turned and saw Walter. He said very loudly and with some glee in his voice, "There is the *real doctor!*" In that split second, I knew that if I stayed, no matter how prominent I might become, he would always be the "real doctor."

I lost my role model, my mentor and respected friend when Walter McBride died at age 96. Now, as I look back through the tube of time, I have to agree with that young patient. *Walter McBride was the* real *doctor.*

One That Wouldn't Leave

One afternoon as I practiced in the "quiet" surroundings of my pedodontic practice, I heard the screaming and crying of a child patient in the dental office directly below me. The noise continued for at least twenty minutes before it stopped. A few minutes after the disturbance ceased, I heard footsteps in my reception room. Then I heard my receptionist making an appointment for the obstreperous child who had just unnerved Dr. Doe, who practiced in that office below.

Shortly after they left with an appointment, Dr. Doe came in and said, "Mel, I sure didn't do you any favors by referring that little @#&*$ to you. I failed, although I used every trick I knew. Good luck."

A few weeks later, I heard a genuine fuss in my reception room. I didn't have to be told who was there. I recognized the screaming. It was a bit of a struggle for the mother and me to get the patient into the chair. He continued to vocally object until I shouted over his noise, "If you don't stop that right now, I'm sending you back down to Dr. Doe."

It worked like a charm. He instantly became cooperative. The mother returned to the reception room. Then I completed the necessary dental procedures on the patient in a friendly manner.

A few days later, I met Dr. Doe in the hall and he inquired about that @#&*$ kid. I stated that I had just learned another technique that could be added to my bag of tricks. He was interested in what that might be.

I related that I had threatened to send the patient back to him and that was all the youngster had to hear!

We had a good laugh over that, but I wonder how many of my peers had been using that same method of child control by saying, "If you don't behave, I'm sending you to Noonan!" If they did, I'll bet it worked.

The Discriminating Patient

A very distinguished African American couple brought their five-year-old daughter to my office for dental treatment. The father, who could have played center for any of the professional football teams, was dressed as though he could have stepped off the pages of *Gentleman's Quarterly*. Both mother and daughter could have been models, too. The only flaw I could see was the condition of the child's dentition. Caries was rampant. A very serious lecture on diet was definitely in order.

After discussing the bad snacks and the healthy diet, the mother said, "What about chocolate milk?" I stated that chocolate milk had a high sugar content and I knew of one study that concluded that chocolate interfered with the metabolism of calcium. Then I said, "Why do you ask? Does she drink a lot of it?"

"Oh, yes. That is all she will drink. She will not touch white milk."

I turned, looked the child straight in the eye, and said, "Why won't you touch white milk? Are you prejudiced?"

For a split second, I thought that might not have been the right thing to say to a child with a father that big; but loud laughter quickly filled the room.

The child did remain a patient for many years after — another case where they *did* come back!

Natural Nutrition — A Cause For Dental Problems

*D*id you ever experience having a thought pop into your head, pass through your vocal cords, ride over your tongue, fly through your lips and into somebody's ear before your inhibitors could react? Well, I have. I think that is what is referred to as "hoof-in-mouth disease."

I recall a buxomly built woman who brought her four-year-old son to my office. The boy presented a perfect example of the "milk bottle" syndrome. Here was my chance to impress the parent with my knowledge.

"Mrs. _____, the reason your child's mouth is in this condition is because you are putting him to bed with a bottle of milk or possibly a sweet fruit juice."

Her answer, which startled me, was, "He never gets a bottle. He sleeps with my husband and me and breast-feeds during the night; but . . . never a bottle."

I replied, "Well, he might not get a bottle, but the result of having the milk in his mouth all night is causing the problem — rampant tooth decay."

Then, in a defensive mood, she stated, "Sometimes he takes water."

At that point, I made my Freudian slip. "Lady — you have me completely confused. Do you mind telling me which one is milk and which one is water?"

Now, if I end this story with "they never came back," you will get the impression that I never kept any patients. This one also stayed.

After we both had a good, hearty laugh, the patient was reappointed and I completed the necessary operative work. I never did find out which one was which, but I will readily admit that I have often wondered what arrangements they made for the boy when he left home for college!

What Did *You* Do In The War?

A few years ago, the American Dental Association (ADA) developed the project "Select." Its object was to have its members seek out and encourage young people who they thought would be good material and qualified for the profession to go for it. Who is more qualified to inspire students to dentistry than the dentist? And as such, we represent a very well-respected segment of the health-care team.

I relate a personal experience where I influenced a fine young man to seek a career with a D.D.S. degree.

One evening when our son, Brian, was eight years old, he greeted me excitedly upon my return home from another day of wet finger dentistry. You didn't have to be a genius to know what the conversation was in the third grade that day by the question he asked.

"Dad, how many Germans did you kill in the war?"

"Brian, I know you want me to be honest. The truth is, none."

A disappointed expression covered his face as he thought for a moment or two. "Well, how many Japanese did you shoot?"

"None. All of the three years I served in the army, I served as a dentist in this country. A dentist in the service is considered a non-combatant. They are not even issued a gun. No, son, I never shot any of the enemy nor anyone else and I pray to God I never do kill."

Again there was a long pause and his expression was one displaying deep concentration. Then he hugged me and stated, "I'm going to be a dentist too, because I never want to kill either."

So, almost thirty years later, I can feel very proud and brag about the person I influenced to study dentistry — our son, Brian.

Patient Turnoffs

*I*t is easy to establish goodwill with your patients, but just as easy to break down the positive relationship you've established. Dynamic Dental Strategies and ADA marketing newsletter listed eight common patient turnoffs. These tips are applicable to most human interactions, in and out of the workplace.

1. Talking about, not to, the patient. Especially true of children, but affecting adults as well, this tendency on the part of the dental team makes the most important person — the patient — feel left out.

2. Ignoring the patient at the reception desk. The patient should be greeted by the receptionist on the way in and on the way out, and should not have to wait to pay or schedule the next appointment.

3. Forgetting that the patient can see and hear practically everything happening in the dental office. If you need to discuss practice management problems with the staff, hold these discussions in private; not in the operatory.

4. Gossiping in front of the patient. Don't talk about other patients or other staff members in front of patients. They'll wonder what you say about them when they leave!

5. Not answering the phone promptly. Patients expect you to be organized and ready to receive phone calls.

6. Forgetting the patient's name — or misspelling it — or mispronouncing it.

7. Failing to inform before you perform. A considerable amount of anxiety on the patient's part can be avoided if he or she understands the next step before it happens.

8. Sending mixed signals on fees and payment options. If the back office and front office send the patient different messages, the entire office lacks credibility.

SECTION FOUR

A BRIEF LOOK AT MY TENURE WITH OCDS

Misinterpreted Humor

*D*id you ever feel that you said something humorous and thought it would be accepted as such, but it wasn't? Certainly, it is a common occurrence to all of us. Not only what you say, but how you say it, can be misinterpreted.

It seems to me that I have had more than my share of such episodes. I had hardly settled into the chair as the executive director of Oakland County Dental Society (OCDS) when the telephone rang. After a formal greeting, the lady on the other end of the line asked if I could refer her to an adult dentist.

With a twinkle in my eye, which of course she could not see, I replied, "Lady, every dentist I know is an adult."

Evidently, this woman did not have the sense of humor I had hoped for. There was a small pause and, with elevated voice, she said, "I'll call back when I don't have to speak to a smart ass." Bang went the phone.

I felt terrible to think that she had taken offense to my remark. I didn't even get a chance to apologize.

Within five minutes, the phone rang again. "This is the Oakland County Dental Society, Dr. Noonan." Another bang! The phone on the other end of the line slammed down again.

I was sure it was the same lady I had just spoken with. Was it her motive to speak to a member of the board of directors and have me fired? If that happened, I would have set a record for having the shortest term as director of this outfit.

That was almost ten years ago, so she didn't report me. However, now that I have confessed, there may still be a chance that they will destroy my contract.

This One Angers Slowly

Over the years in my position as executive director, I have received quite a few complaints against dentists. Most of these are frivolous and caused by lack of communication between the patient and doctor. Other cases are initiated after the dentist tries to collect a delinquent account. They may have had no complaint up to this point. For them, paying the bill is unpleasant . . . so complain.

But one of the most bizarre cases registered in this office was a man who wanted a dentist investigated. His story went like this:

The dentist restored a tooth and the patient claimed he heard him tell his assistant, "I placed that one really deep; he'll be back for a root canal and then a crown."

I told the complainant that it was difficult for me to believe that any practitioner in his right mind would make such a statement in earshot of a patient.

Over a short period of time, he had the same dentist insert four more restorations. Eventually all five teeth needed root canal therapy and crowns.

It seems that any person with an ounce of wit would have changed practitioners before he needed the fifth crown.

The man was insistent in what he had overheard, and readily divulged the doctor's name.

I inquired when all this took place (you will not believe his answer).

"Seventeen years ago."

After giving him a verbal pat on the head, I informed him that this case definitely was beyond the statute of limitations and nothing could be accomplished now.

This fellow has to be a "slow burner." He felt he needed a little time to think about it before he complained.

The Female Professional

A s we age, our thoughts, priorities, and philosophies change along with numerous physical alterations.

Our views take on different perspectives as we grow older. We mellow. On one subject, FEMALE DENTISTS, I have mellowed.

A few years back, I felt very strongly that accepting a female into dental school was a complete waste. Each one that was accepted just closed a space for a male.

After graduation, if not already, they would marry, have babies, and disappear from the work force in a very short time — a total loss of energy and money. Not much of a contribution to the oral health of the public.

If instead they had admitted a man for the spot, he would have been able to supply his services for many more years. Therefore, a greater valuable asset to the community.

I hate to admit (at least publicly) that I was wrong. But I will scrape up the courage and say, "I was wrong."

In my position as executive director of a dental association, I have had my eyes and mind opened. I am amazed at the amount of energy that our female members possess. They compete with their male counterparts, attain a very respectable position in class standings, practice excellent dentistry, have their babies, return to practice and get involved in organized dentistry. They accept responsibility and do their assignments with professionalism.

To those of the feminine gender, my sentiments are taken from a cigarette advertisement: "You have come a long way, Baby!" God bless you.

This Is a True Story

Getting involved with the final plans for the Oakland County Dental Society's annual golf outing one year, there came to mind several stories that golfers might enjoy. Hopefully, those not interested in the game will forgive me for bringing up the subject.

> Two elderly members of the Birmingham [Michigan] Country Club were engaged in a little match. According to their own rules, the most either could lose was $4.00, which both could well afford. One was a physician; the other a lawyer. Although they were very good friends, neither would give the other a one-inch putt.

On the sixth hole, the attorney drove off and hit the fairway. The physician drove his ball into the rough. The lawyer had it spotted and started for that area to help the doctor find it.

While he was searching for it, he heard his opponent yell, "Here it is!"

When he turned, he saw the medic address and hit a ball from the fairway. He was certain that the ball his opponent just hit was not the one either had hit from the tee!

Sure enough, he spotted the original ball in the tall grass and he called out, "That ball you just hit was not the one you hit off the tee."

The response from the good doctor: "Yes it is, but you just found a brand-new Titleist 2."

You can bet the barrister won that hole!

SECTION FIVE
ET CETERA . . .

A Difficult Loss —
An Important Lesson

*I*n previous stories, I have told you how I have lost patients. I hope that you have found these stories amusing and have been able to relate to some of my experiences. But as I write this, I find myself in a very somber mood. I have lost a very good friend who was never a patient.

I first met "Pete" while I was performing the duties of a special examiner for the Michigan State Board of Dentistry. He was a candidate for a specialty license in pediatric dentistry. He passed the challenge with flying colors, demonstrating an exceptional talent in the operative phase and a 90 percent score in theory.

Through the ensuing years, our paths crossed many times and our friendship grew. We shared a mutual respect and admiration for each other.

He started his practice in the western part of the state and gained an excellent reputation in a short time. His practice grew to the point where he could easily afford a well-maintained farm, which included his dearly loved horses.

He had it made. From his peak he could see nothing but sunshine. All was well until he developed an eye problem that at first was improperly diagnosed. After several failed treatments, a proper diagnosis was made, but all too late; he lost the eye.

Pete was crushed. He had no depth perception and could no longer practice dentistry. In the physical sense, that was tragedy enough; but the mental trauma was much worse.

Thankfully, prior to his loss he had planned well. He had purchased adequate disability insurance and a good estate plan. So, from a financial view, he was protected and his family did have monetary security. Although these facts would lessen one's mental stress, it never helped him.

Several of his peers and I offered to help. We tried to encourage him to use his knowledge in some other area of dentistry not requiring operative skills. We failed. Even professional counseling failed. He turned, as so many others have in the time of a crisis, to the "glass crutch." This habit can take one to cheap bars where one will find cheap women. The chain reaction continues until a marriage and home are broken.

Give him credit — he tried. He tried desperately at times to regain stability; he never did. Just recently, he ended it all with a device designed for self-protection, not self-destruction.

Dentistry has lost a great human resource. All of us who knew and worked with him will feel the void. In our minds, the question, "What else could we have done?" will remain for a long time.

Why do I tell this story? I do it with the hope that it will prevent another such tragedy.

In case of such misfortune, minimize the mental stress by keeping your house in order. Have adequate disability insurance and keep your estate plans current. Secondly, remember that there are groups within organized dentistry[1] willing to help dentists involved in substance abuse. In Michigan, it is known as Dr. Care. They do their job in the strictest confidential manner. Although it did not prevent my friend from taking his life, it might help someone close to you. They do not lose many.

1. I hope readers will adapt this message to any group to which they may belong. There is always help for anyone.

Marketing . . . And An Afterthought

*I*n today's business world, marketing is a very vital ingredient. Colleges and universities offer degrees on the subject. There is a vast field of opportunity for those who excel in that area. It is also true that not all marketing is quality marketing. Some can be rated as poor, ineffective, and even irritating. To be specific, there is the annoying phone call made right around dinner time. The perpetrator is confident that you will be available at that moment, and doesn't mind interrupting your meal.

Recently, I had that experience. A call came during dinner and the conversation went like this:

"Hello."

"May I speak to Melvin Noonan."

"You are speaking to Melvin Noonan."

"How are you, Melvin?"

"Fine."

"This is Jane Doe. I'm calling to tell you that you have been selected to receive three free dance lessons from _____ _____ Dance Studio."

"With one leg?" I replied (I really do have two).

"Oh! I'm sorry; please excuse the call."

I was proud of the fact that I was able to cut the conversation short and return to my dinner.

But you must realize that the person on the other end is trying to make a living. She is being paid to make sure she contacts you to make a sale.

The thought came to mind that I could have helped by telling her that if another contact she makes may, indeed, only have one leg, she should say, "So what — that's no excuse. Remember Peg Leg Pete."

~

Always Consider
The Circumstances

Sexual harassment is a hot topic today, and always should have been. Trying to define what constitutes sexual harassment might be rather easy if not considering the circumstances. In other words, there might be a grey area which may or may not make a situation objectionable. One situation I recall could have been classified as harassment, but definitely was not. It was humorous, and both parties agreed.

One of our past presidents, the late George Marin, had a wonderful sense of humor, second to none. He had advertised for a dental hygienist at a time when they were scarce.

In response to his ad, a very beautiful woman responded, and made an appointment for an interview. She very easily could have qualified for the Miss America competition, along with having all the qualifications of a good hygienist.

At the appointed hour, George stepped into the reception room and there she was. He took one look and said, "I don't care if you can clean teeth or not. You are hired."

That set a record for the shortest job interview in the State of Michigan.

Some may consider that harassment, but it wasn't. They worked together for many years without harassment raising its ugly head.

An Important Aspect of Being in Business

*P*reviously, I mentioned how I was impressed by the ADA Select Program and how I influenced our son, Brian, to follow a career in the profession of dentistry. You might think I would be content and expand my chest, saying, "There, I did my part." But, no. I have started to work on a grandson, Timmy, age 12.

Timmy mentioned to his grandmother that he had to find a job that would pay him $100. When she asked why, he stated that he needed it to join a swim club or go on a trip to Mackinac Island.

When my wife related the story to me, I decided to talk to him. "Timmy, I heard you were looking for a job. If that be the case, I have just the job for you. You can paint the playhouse and I'll pay you."

"I'll paint the playhouse, but you don't have to pay me, Grandpa."

"No, Timmy. I'm willing to pay you. I would have to pay somebody else to do it."

"Well, how much would you pay?"

"Fifteen dollars an hour."

"Fifteen dollars? Gee, that's a lot!"

"Well, Timmy, you will be staying overnight; will you not?"

"Yes."

"And you will be getting your meals; right?"

"Yes."

"Well, after those expenses are deducted, it will figure out to be $1.25 profit for you."

How will that influence him? I'm not sure, but I thought if he gets an idea that he wants to get into the profession, he better learn early what overhead is all about.

(P.S. He did paint the playhouse and did make *more* than $1.25 an hour.)

We Never Had a Favorite

*W*ith the holiday season at hand, I felt the following story would be appropriate, providing you excuse the intimate personal touch.

When Dwight Eisenhower was elected president of the

United States, his mother was asked what she thought of her son. She responded, "Which one?" That meant to me that her mother's love held each of her children as equals, regardless of their position in life.

Each of our three sons was very special to my wife, Laurene, and me. We can honestly say we never had a favorite. We made every effort to treat them equally at all times.

One Christmas when their ages ranged from 7 to 13, we placed a $20 bill in three separate cards and inscribed in each, "To our favorite son." The cards were placed among their other gifts.

On Christmas morning, they went about the task of opening their gifts with great enthusiasm. Brian was the first to open the card. His eyes lit up when he saw the twenty-dollar bill, but he closed the card quickly when he read the inscription. He wanted to protect his brothers' feelings and not let them see that he was selected as our favorite.

His action did not go unnoticed by Tim and Tom, so curiosity had them reach for and open their cards. Looking at one another and noticing the grins on our faces, they realized what we had accomplished . . . letting each know he was our favorite.

Brian seized the opportunity to tease the other two and said, "Gee, Mom and Dad, thanks for the fifty dollars."

"Fifty dollars?" the others cried, and wrestled with him to see his bill.

With proof that his was only twenty also, they knew all of them were on equal footing. They shared equal love then and since.

We always recall that incident during the Yuletide and then deposit it again in our memory bank of happy years gone by.

I Confess

I am certain that all legal opinions would agree that a period of 52 + years would be considered beyond the statute of limitations. With that in mind and feeling safe from malpractice litigation, I'll relate the following experience I had as a dental officer in the United States Army during World War II.

In 1944, Camp Ritchie, Maryland, was the Military Intelligence Training Center for the United States. As a dentist at that post, one had to serve not only our troops, but also German and Italian prisoners of war.

Although the dental staff treated each patient humanely, they had little sympathy for the POWs. One could become somewhat bitter and hardened when hearing stories of brutality as told by returning troops who had been disengaged from some of their body parts which still remained somewhere on the battlefield.

One of the prisoner patients assigned to me was a high-ranking German general. He had a broken bridge on the lower arch and I was ordered to replace it.

Dental gold had been rationed and was to be used only in special cases. Feeling patriotic, I decided to save what gold was available for one of our own, but I did make the bridge. It cost me 40 cents. I melted four dimes and cast the bridge.

Coin silver will take on a great luster. The finished product looked great, fit well, had good occlusion, and pleased the general. After shaking my hand and patting my back, he left with a smile.

I never saw him after that, but would like to have followed him to see how long it took to have my 40-cent investment turn green.

Yes . . . confession is good for the soul!

About the Author

*M*elvin A. Noonan is a native Detroiter and a graduate of Western High School. At a very early age he developed a great interest in dentistry. Although he was orphaned at eighteen years of age, his determination and efforts allowed him to reach that goal.

He received his D.D.S. degree from the University of Detroit in 1943. After a three-year tour with the U.S. Army Dental Corps, he pursued a M.S. degree in pediatric dentistry at the University of Michigan. He established his specialty practice in Birmingham, Michigan.

He has served as president of the Michigan Society of Dentistry for Children; the Oakland County Dental Society; Michigan Academy of Pediatric Dentistry; Kenneth A. Easlick Graduate Society; and the American Academy of Pediatric Dentistry.

He is a diplomate of the American Board of Pediatric Dentistry. He holds Fellowships in the American College of Dentists, the International College of Dentists, and the Pierre Fauchard Academy. He served as the Executive Director of the Oakland County Dental Society for ten years.

He and his wife, Laurene, have three sons; Timothy, Brian, and Thomas; and eight grandchildren.

He claims that God always had him in the right place at the right time.

Order Information

Order *They Never Came Back* from your bookstore.

If unavailable at your bookstore, please send $12.95 plus $2.50 for shipping and handling. Add $.50 for each additional book. Quantity discounts are available. Please contact the publisher.

Michigan residents please add 6% sales tax.

Send _____ book(s).

PLEASE PRINT

Name: _____

Address: _____

_____

City: _____

State: _____ Zip:_____

Telephone:_____

Send check or money order (payable to *Timbritom Press*) plus above information to:

Timbritom Press
P.O. Box 802
Birmingham, MI 48012-0802
(248) 646-7672

THEY NEVER CAME BACK

Cover design by Eric Norton
Text design by Mary Jo Zazueta
in Galliard ITC
Printed by Data Reproductions on
55 lb. Wassau Book Natural
Bound by Dekker Bookbinding
Client Liaison: Theresa Nelson
Production Editor: Alex Moore